MANATEES

SEA MONSTERS

HOMER SEWARD

The Rourke Press, Inc.
Vero Beach, Florida 32964

PHOTO CREDITS
© Marty Snyderman: cover, pages 6, 9, 10, 15, 16, 21, 22;
© Lynn M. Stone: pages 4, 7, 12, 13, 18, 19

EDITORIAL SERVICES:
Penworthy Learning Systems

Library of Congress Cataloging-in-Publication Data

Seward, Homer. 1942-
    Manatees / by Homer Seward.
        p. cm. — (Sea monsters)
    Includes index
    Summary: Introduces manatees, their physical appearance, habits, babies, and status as endangered species.
    ISBN 1-57103-237-1
    1. Manatees—Juvenile literature. [1. Manatees. 2. Endangered species] I. Title. II. Series: Seward, Homer, 1942-   Sea monsters.
QL737.S63S48 1998
599.55—dc21
                                                                98–24062
                                                                    CIP
                                                                     AC

Printed in the USA

TABLE OF CONTENTS

MANATEES

Manatees look like big gray barrels with flippers. Their smooth, round shape helps them swim easily. Manatees spend their whole lives in water.

Manatees live much like fish, but they're **mammals** (MAM ulz), like us. Like all mammals, manatees breathe air. They reach air by swimming to the surface and opening their nostrils just above the waterline.

Manatees have hair, like other mammals, but not much. Manatees raise their babies on mother's milk.

A West Indian manatee loafs in the clear, spring-fed water of Florida's Homosassa River.

MANATEES AS SEA MONSTERS

Sailors long ago may have mistaken manatees for mermaids, if not sea monsters. Early sailors must have been terribly confused by these swimming barrels with the square snouts.

A diver scratches a curious manatee in a Florida river.

A manatee calf nurses on mother's milk, like any young mammal would do.

Far from being monsters—or mermaids— manatees are gentle. They have no natural enemies, so they act like they have nothing to fear. Still, a 1,000-pound (454-kilogram) manatee can be a bit frightening to someone in a canoe or kayak.

WHAT A MANATEE LOOKS LIKE

Up close, a manatee doesn't look at all like a mermaid! The manatee's snout fits on a small head with small eyes. The manatee's upper lip is unusual because it is divided. Each half of the lip can move by itself!

The manatee has a flat tail. It looks and works like a wide paddle. The tail pumps up and down to push the manatee through the water.

The manatee has no rear flippers. What might have been legs or flippers make up its tail. The two front flippers are used to scratch, touch, and hold other manatees.

A manatee loafs in clear, spring-fed water.

WHERE MANATEES LIVE

The manatee likes fairly warm water. In the United States, it lives mostly in the waters along Florida's coasts.

During the warmest months, many manatees travel north to Georgia. Sometimes they swim as far as Virginia. They also travel along the Gulf Coast to Texas.

Manatees use both salt water and fresh water. In winter, they often swim into Florida's warm, spring-fed rivers, like the Crystal River. They also loaf in the pools of warm water that power plants create.

A diver swims with a manatee in the Crystal River.

HABITS OF MANATEES

Manatees may stay in one place for a few days, weeks, or even months. When the water becomes too cold or food is scarce, they move on.

Manatees live on greens. A big manatee will eat over 100 pounds (45 kilograms) of manatee "salad" every day!

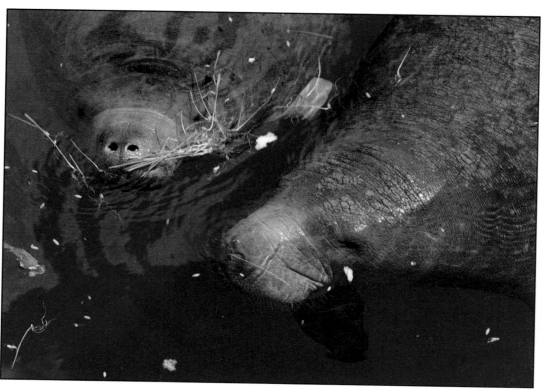

Manatees munch aquatic plants. Adults can eat over 100 pounds of greens daily.

A manatee pops its snout above the surface to catch a breath of air.

Manatees gobble plants on the surface and plants underwater down to 12 feet (4 meters).

Manatees hear very well. A mother manatee will scream—underwater, of course—to call her calf. Manatees also chirp and squeal to one another.

BABY MANATEES

Baby manatees are born underwater. They must quickly swim to the surface for their first breath.

A newborn calf weighs about 70 pounds (32 kilograms). It learns quickly—within a half day—to swim and breathe without mom's help.

The baby lives on mother's milk for about a month. It then begins taking a few plants along with the milk.

A young manatee leaves its mother at the age of one or two years. It won't have a calf of its own until it's eight or nine years old.

A manatee cow swims with its baby, known as a calf.

THE MANATEE'S COUSINS

The manatee belongs to a group of **aquatic** (uh KWAT ik) mammals called **sirens** (SY rens). Aquatic animals of any kind spend most or all their lives in water. Whales are also aquatic mammals.

The manatee of America is the West Indian manatee. A second **species** (SPEE sheez), or kind, of manatee lives in West Africa.

The Amazon manatee lives in fresh water in South America. The dugong of Asia, Africa, and Australia is a close cousin of the manatee.

The largest of the sirens was the 22,000-pound (about 10,000-kilogram) Steller's sea cow of the icy Bering Sea. It became **extinct** (eks TINKT) in 1768.

Manatees are sirens, aquatic mammals that, like whales, spend their entire lives in water.

MANATEES AND PEOPLE

Manatees are harmless, but one habit gets them in trouble with people anyway. Manatees usually swim close to the surface of the water. That makes them easy targets for meat hunters in Mexico and Caribbean Sea nations.

People enjoy watching or swimming with manatees, but people's speeding boats have injured and killed hundreds of manatees.

Lending a helping hand, a park attendant at Florida's Homosassa Springs feed injured and orphaned manatees.

In the United States, manatees are not table food. But they are often struck and sometimes killed by the propellers of boats.

The West Indian manatee has become rare. The total number in Florida is probably no more than 1,200.

SAVING MANATEES

Manatees are **endangered** (en DAYN jerd). That means they are in danger of becoming extinct, or disappearing forever, like the sea cow.

Manatees in the United States are protected by the laws of the U.S. Government. Signs warn boaters when they are in a known manatee area.

By reducing boat speed, a boater gives the manatee a chance to dive out of the way. Even so, scientists can tell one manatee from another by its boat scars.

Signs posted on Florida waterways ask boaters to slow down for the safety of manatees.

GLOSSARY

aquatic (uh KWAT ik) — of the water; living on or in the water

endangered (en DAYN jerd) — in danger of no longer existing; very rare

extinct (eks TINKT) — to no longer exist; the complete disappearance of a living plant or animal species

mammal (MAM ul) — a group of warm-blooded animals that produce milk, have hair, breathe air, and usually have four limbs

siren (SY ren) — a small family of marine mammals that eat plants, have two front flippers and a tail, and live in seas and coastal rivers

species (SPEE sheez) — within a group of closely related animals, one certain kind, such as the *West Indian* manatee

Manatees seem unbothered by the attention of a human in mask and fins.

INDEX

FURTHER READING

Find out more about manatees with these helpful books:
Burton, John. *Mammals of North America.* Thunder Bay, 1995.
McNulty, Faith. *Dancing with Manatees.* Scholastic, 1994.
Palmer, Sarah. *Manatees.* Rourke 1989.